Keeping It Together

IN A PULL-APART WORLD

Keeping It Together

IN A PULL-APART WORLD

Mary Ellen Edmunds

DESERET BOOK

SALT LAKE CITY, UTAH

Text © 2007 Mary Ellen Edmunds
Illustrations © 2007 Aaron Taylor

Visit us at DeseretBook.com

Library of Congress Cataloging-in-Publication Data
Edmunds, Mary Ellen, 1940-
  Keeping it together in a pull-apart world / Mary Ellen Edmunds.
    p.   cm.
    ISBN-13: 978-1-59038-754-2 (hardback : alk. paper)
  1. Christian life—Mormon authors.   2. Stress (Psychology)—Religious
aspects—Church of Jesus Christ of Latter-day Saints. I. Title.
  BX8656.E35 2007
  248.4'89332—dc22   2007009331

Printed in Mexico
R. R. Donnelley and Sons, Reynosa, Mexico
10   9   8   7   6   5   4   3   2   1

To the MBAs of the TOFW Village:
Thanks for reducing stress through
your friendship, wisdom, kindness, and
wild humor—you know who you are!

The "S" Monsters

HOW DO YOU RESPOND when you hear the word "stress" or the phrase "stressed out"? What happens to your pulse, your blood pressure, your skin, your breathing, or your internal scream mechanism (ISM) when you even *think* about stress?

How do you cope with stress? How do you talk yourself INTO it, and how do you talk yourself OUT of it?

Did it get your attention when I asked how you talk yourself INTO it? Why would anyone ever talk herself or himself into feeling stressed?

But we do, don't we? I can see by the look on your face (yes, I'm watching you as you're reading) that you sometimes do this. I do too.

It's a common problem. We get overcome by the "S" Monsters: The Shoulds and the Shouldn'ts. Do any of the following examples sound familiar?

I should have done more yesterday—weeded the garden, organized my food supply, polished my CTR ring.

I shouldn't have eaten the snacks that had been prepared for the children in the nursery.

I should get out of debt, be a better parent, wife, friend, sister, and neighbor, show love to all my children, and be a constant example of generosity, dignity, inner peace, courage, beauty, and unselfishness.

I shouldn't have been quite so brutally honest when Fifi asked me how she looked in her new outfit.

I should have made a prioritized list for tomorrow.

I shouldn't have put my to-do lists in the shredder.

I should be keeping a journal, making dazzling scrapbooks, writing more letters, doing more visiting of the sick and afflicted and those who have cause to mourn.

I shouldn't have put Jon's BlackBerry in his scripture bag.

I should exercise, floss, consume fresh fruits and veggies six times a day, clean the basement, and keep the laundry caught up.

I shouldn't have been so hard on Alyssa when she flunked geometry—like I have a master's in math or something!

I should memorize the *Ensign* and the "Tropical Guide," complete my visiting teaching early, attend more meetings, and ponder.

I probably shouldn't have given ALL the video games to D.I.

I should never feel hurt . . . I should always be happy and serene, control my temper better, be extraordinarily patient, be totally self-reliant, and never get tired or sick or ugly or succumb to road rage.

I shouldn't have bitten my neighbor's cat after that incident last week.

I should pray more earnestly, go to the temple more often, and do tons of family history work.

I shouldn't go shopping when I'm hungry, or without a list, or without coupons.

I should be trustworthy, loyal, helpful, friendly, courteous, kind, obedient, cheerful, thrifty, brave, clean, and reverent. (And I should be a Silver Beaver . . . or at least an Eagle Scout!)

Maybe I shouldn't have said no to tending the grandkids again, this time for two weeks while John and Mary are in Hawaii.

I should run for public office, learn to change the oil in my car, volunteer to help with literacy at the library, and study the Dead Sea Scrolls.

I shouldn't have hidden the Froot Loops in my closet.

Take a breath! I promise not to list anything else! (But you *know* I could.)

By now you should have the idea: I think we bring a lot of stress on ourselves by being, as some say, "our own worst enemies." We come up with a lot of our very own "shoulds" and "should nots." And the resulting stress can be awful.

A Stressful Morning

HAVE YOU EVER HAD A morning when you just knew you were off to such a good start and organized so well that it would be a spectacular day of incredible accomplishments? That's the way I was feeling early one beautiful morning a while ago.

I was on my way to take my mother to get her hair cut. Simple. And I'd left early enough to get a couple of things done on my way. No problem.

I was right on schedule, and everything was hunky-dory. (Is that really an appropriate way to describe anything at all?)

But . . . I didn't plan on the train—the LONG train bringing coal from Carbon County. Uh-oh.

And I didn't count on the lady with her arms full of packages running ahead of me at the post office, plopping her packages down on the counter of the one open window, and going out to the car for MORE. Uh-oh.

And I didn't count on the older man behind me in line who asked sweetly, "Having fun yet?" How could I not have responded to that, to him?

"Yes!" I said. "I've been up since before 2:30, and I've had some good fun!"

So he began talking about his hobby of making beautiful things from wood scraps. He in fact followed me out of the post office and showed me a loose-leaf binder filled with pictures of

projects he'd done or was working on, from cup-
boards to knickknack shelves to . . . Uh-oh.

I finally told him I really had to leave and
asked if he had a card. He did.

Well, Mom missed her appointment.
Interestingly, just a couple of days before that she
had told my brother John (with whom she lives):
"If Mary Ellen is going to take me somewhere,
she is ALWAYS early."

And I almost always am. Except for this particular September morning.

Okay, it wasn't the end of the world. I probably
should have called this a "stress lite" experience. But ·
it truly caused me to feel stressed out.

So what did I do on the stressful morning
when I made my mother miss her appointment to
get her hair cut? I took her instead to visit her
grandson James, who had just received a kidney
from his father (my brother Frank) a week before.
(On a side note, Frank, who recently became a

bishop, might be sending out from his ward one of his own sons pretty soon. Blessings!)

Can I just say that thinking about that put a whole lot of other things—like a long train, a package queen, and a wood-carver—in a different light?

When we got back to drop Mom off at home, I spent some time in the backyard with Jack, age one. I just played with him. And as I eventually buckled him into a car-seat type swing and pushed him gently over and over and over . . . he went to sleep, and the stress drained out of me.

I'm going to make a guess that someone reading this might be thinking: "That doesn't sound at all familiar. Let Edmunds be a single mom on an important conference call with her boss and some clients (yes, while driving), and put three screaming kids in car seats in the back of a van with peanut butter and jelly sandwiches, and *then* we can talk stress!"

Or someone might read about my morning and think. "Oh, to be sitting there in my car just watching a train go by—just to have a moment where I'm *stopped*."

We don't all have the very same things going on in our lives, do we? But I think most of us understand what stress feels like.

You might have circumstances that go way beyond the scope of what I will attempt to cover in this little book. Perhaps you're dealing with divorce, abuse, chronic illness, addiction, children or parents with long-term disabilities, a spouse who has lost faith, a family member who struggles with a mental illness, the loss of a loved one, or any number of other very heavy burdens.

Even though there may not be specific answers to some of your biggest questions, I sincerely hope that some of the ideas we'll share here will be helpful to you in some way.

A Pull-Apart World

HAVE YOU NOTICED, as I have, how ours is becoming more and more a pull-apart world? There is so much that seems to make us competitive with and distant from our neighbors, our fellow travelers—even from the very ones who could help lift and lighten our burdens.

I collect advertisements that illustrate what I've been observing. One of them boasts this as its slogan: "Separate yourself from the rest of humanity!" Ouch!

It's almost as if we're being pulled away from ourselves, too—from our cores, our spirits, our

best selves, our souls. Have you had moments when you've hardly recognized yourself—when you've thought something like: "Was that me?" "Did I really do that?" "Did I actually say that?" "What's happening!" Such moments have happened to me far too frequently. I'm making progress, but I still do and say some ridiculous things.

Have you had moments when you've hardly recognized yourself—when you've thought something like: "Did I really do that?"

I've thought a lot about our challenges, our busy-ness, the pace of life (which seems to be increasing as the years go by, and even as the hours go by!), the collection of lists of things that must be done last week, last month, or tomorrow.

Ah, yes, the List Collection. (Doesn't it sound like a line of beautiful towels or something?) There's that tangible evidence that we haven't lived up to our intentions.

I ran across the following statement by President Ezra Taft Benson (and this was more than thirty years ago!): "We live in an age when, as the Lord foretold, men's hearts are failing them, not only physically but in spirit. (See D&C 45:26.) . . . As the showdown between good and evil approaches with its accompanying trials and tribulations, Satan is increasingly striving to overcome the Saints with despair, discouragement, despondency, and depression" (*Ensign,* November 1974, 65).

Do you recognize those feelings in your own heart and life—feelings of despair, discouragement, despondency, and depression? Do you sometimes feel burned out, stressed out, irritable, weary . . . empty?

What IS stress? Simply put, stress is our response, our reaction, to what's happening around us.

Stress can actually be a motivator. If you've ever written a term paper the night before it was due, you know what I'm talking about.

Stress can actually be a motivator. If you've ever written a term paper the night before it was due, you know what I'm talking about.

But generally, I think that a little bit of stress goes a long, long way. My feeling is that although stress may be a FACT of life, it needn't be a WAY of life.

Ask yourself the following questions slowly, thinking about your answers:

How long has it been since you really *relaxed* at home . . . since you just sat, without feeling restless and guilty?

How long has it been since you drove anywhere without being in a hurry, and without feeling frustrated?

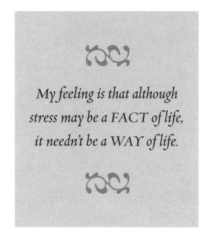

My feeling is that although stress may be a FACT of life, it needn't be a WAY of life.

How long has it been since you wrote in your journal after a busy day or week: "And it came to pass that we lived after the manner of happiness" (as Nephi did; see 2 Nephi 5:27).

I read about a teacher who was explaining stress management to his students. He raised a glass of water and asked, "How heavy is this glass of water?" Answers ranged from A to Z. The teacher said that the absolute weight didn't matter. It depended on how long you tried to hold it.

"If I hold it for a minute, that's not a problem. If I hold it for an hour, I'll have an ache in my right arm. If I hold it for a day, you'll have to call an ambulance. In each case, it's the same weight, but the longer I hold it, the heavier it becomes."

And that's a pretty good illustration of what happens with stress, isn't it? If we carry our burdens all the time, sooner or later, as the burden becomes increasingly heavy, we won't be able to carry it anymore. We have to put it down for a while, or maybe allow others to help bear our burdens, to help make them lighter and more bearable. We need to have some periods of rest.

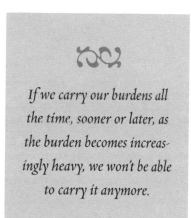

If we carry our burdens all the time, sooner or later, as the burden becomes increasingly heavy, we won't be able to carry it anymore.

Ideas for Keeping It Together

THIS IDEA OF FINDING some rest, of keeping it together in our pull-apart world has been *much* on my mind, because I think we're missing a lot by being stressed out so much of the time. Life is short. I'm feeling we ought to enjoy it more.

I have a big badge that says, "Enjoy life—this is not a dress rehearsal!" I'd like to see if I can help you think of ways you *can* enjoy life—ways you can reduce the stress and the busy-ness, the frantic pace of the hours and the days. I'm going to suggest some ways for us to put our burdens down for a moment or two, as that's possible, and rest and relax.

I realize that as you read you might feel like there's nothing "new" here—and maybe there isn't—but I hope you find one or two or more ideas that you've not tried in a while. The ideas aren't given in any particular order, and it certainly isn't my intent that you do them all at once. That would really stress you out! Just pick something that you think might work for you today.

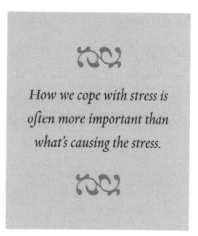

How we cope with stress is often more important than what's causing the stress.

Interestingly, how we *cope* with stress is often more important than what's *causing* the stress. And yet I list this as the first suggestion in dealing with stress:

♥ *As much as you can, find out what is causing you to feel stressed out.*

I pretty much do this automatically these days. "Edmunds," I'll ask myself, "what's going on? What is it?" For me it makes a difference if I can identify what is making me feel stressed. It's easier to tackle the known than the unknown.

♥ *Take one thing at a time.*

I've talked to many others who feel the same way I do—that when you're trying to work on, solve, and finish everything at once, there is more tendency to feel stress. Perhaps we could call this "scatter stress." Or "skeewampus stress." Or "chicken-with-its-head-off" stress. And there are situations where that's just the

It's easier to tackle the known than the unknown.

way it is. But when you *can,* try taking one thing at a time. It's like the response to the question, "How do you eat an elephant?" "One bite at a time."

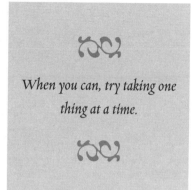

When you can, try taking one thing at a time.

When I'm working on a Big Project, sometimes I say to myself, "You're an ant" (not to be confused with being an aunt). "Just keep plodding forward with your little load, and then you can come back for more." I'm reminding myself that little accomplishments begin to add up.

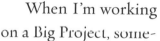*Claim back some of your lost hours.*

Could you maybe cut out one or two TV shows? Glance through only one or two catalogues? Do you recognize that you spend too much time talking on the phone, or reading nonsense? See what you can do to trim some of the "fat" from your too-busy schedule. My friend Whit sets a timer for some activities, and when the timer goes off, she stops. Would that work for you?

♥ *Recognize that there are things you cannot control or change.*

This might include your age (although many try to "control" aging in all kinds of interesting ways), the weather, or the number of hours in a day. You probably can't change how long you have to sit in the waiting room for an appointment, how many drivers have chosen to be on the freeway at the same time as you, how long it takes the line to move, whether the stoplight turns red or green, and so on.

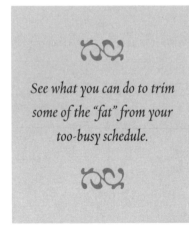

See what you can do to trim some of the "fat" from your too-busy schedule.

💗 *Recognize the things you CAN control or change.*

Focus on these more than on the things you *can't* control and change, and you're likely to feel better. You can control and change your reaction to others, your to-do list (the number of items on the list, and the priority you give to each), your goals, how much time you're willing to spend (invest) in a particular project, the quality of your prayers, how you treat others,

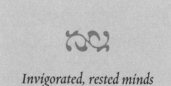

Invigorated, rested minds and bodies do much better in handling stress than do exhausted ones. How about a nap once in a while?

and so on. You can even do things to minimize the stress of waiting for an appointment, waiting in line, waiting in traffic, and other stress-producing circumstances.

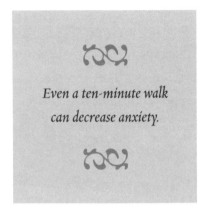

Even a ten-minute walk can decrease anxiety.

❧ *Get a good night's rest.*

Most of us are more easily stressed when we're tired. "Retire to thy bed early, that ye may not be weary; arise early, that your bodies and your minds may be invigorated" (D&C 88:124). Invigorated, rested minds and bodies do much better in handling stress than do exhausted ones. How about a nap once in a while?

❧ *Exercise.*

Exercise clears your mind and returns your body to a more healthful state. Even a ten-minute walk can decrease anxiety. So go for a walk, alone or with someone you enjoy being with. Either way, it can be such a stress reliever. Sometimes when I go alone, early in the morning, I visit with

Heavenly Father about anything and everything. It's a wonderful way to start the day.

❤ *Avoid unnecessary competition.*

I think there's probably a better word than *unnecessary* here, but what I mean is to avoid the competition that creates a pull-apart world. It's too prevalent in our lives, I think—the focus on winning (or making sure our children always win). An unrealistic need to always be *first* can create excessive tension, anxiety, aggression, and terrible disappointment.

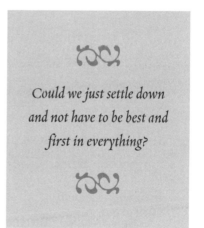

Could we just settle down and not have to be best and first in everything?

Do we too often seem to compare ourselves with and compete against *everybody* about *everything?* How stressful is that! Could we just settle down and not have to be best and first in everything? Remember Paul's analogy (in 1 Corinthians 12), where he teaches that each of us who is a part of the whole is unique, and we each matter. He taught that when one member suffers, all the members suffer with it—but when one member is honored, all the members rejoice with it!

So, even though you really felt it was what *you* wanted to do, let Vivian have her turn in the nursery, and be happy for her! Rejoice with her! We need to come closer together and eliminate that which pulls us apart. Remember: If we each gained ten pounds, we'd all be closer together!

❧ *Become as a child.*

Be real. Are there things about our world, our pull-apart world, that make us feel we have to pretend to be someone we're not? Sometimes it seems that way. There is something so refreshing, so freeing, about being comfortable in our own skin, with our unique way of doing and being. Children are especially good at this!

💗 *Cultivate optimism.*

Consciously become a more positive, optimistic person. I heard a wonderful description of this one time. Upon meeting Goliath, the pessimist says, "He's so HUGE! There is NO WAY I'm going to be able to beat him!" And the optimist? He says, "He's so HUGE! There's NO WAY I can miss!"

💗 *Cut down on clutter.*

Notice that I didn't say get rid of clutter, although in some cases that may be needed. Do you have more "stuff and things" than you have space for (in your *life* as well as in your home, garage, office, apartment, closet, purse, basement, or wherever)? Are you spending more for a storage shed (for your clutter) than for ice cream? Someone once said that a fire is a way to

get rid of clutter quickly and completely . . . but it's certainly not a recommended method. More and more I look at mementos (a *momento* is a Spanish moment, often mistaken for a *memento*) and ask them what they're doing in my home.

I'm giving myself five years to get organized. (See, I really AM an optimist! Only five years!) I hope you never have a chance to talk to anyone who helped me move last year—they know it's going to take at LEAST five years! But I admit I'm making progress.

❤ *Do some cleaning and organizing that's long-lasting.*

Things like doing the laundry, washing dishes, and dusting are things that need to be done over and over. In a way, they're never "done." No such thing as "done" with a lot of things on our list. But does it feel as good to you as it does to me to do something that lasts longer than a day or two? Try cleaning a room, a closet, a drawer, the garage, the basement. Write a letter;

visit someone; complete some family history work. Those are just a few examples of some things that, when completed, can last a little longer, and they can really lift your spirits.

❤ *Become a rock star.*

Get a comfortable rocking chair and put it to work, or just "twitch" occasionally. If you have a Cracker Barrel restaurant nearby, you can use theirs! A rocking motion might just do the trick, calming you down and even giving you some time to meditate a bit.

❤ *Call a friend.*

Be both a talker *and* a listener—take turns. Don't unload so much so often that your friend gets caller ID just to limit or spread out your calls! Maybe we could add to this idea things like text messages and e-mail—other ways to keep in touch.

♥ *Let others help you more often.*

Let's sometimes back away from "No, I'm just fine. Don't worry about me." One of my nephews helped me in my yard for a while. One day he cut through a sprinkler wire. On this occasion I liked my response (many times I've not responded charitably to such things): "Well, it sure looks like a twig to MEE!" His brother came and fixed the wire a few days later.

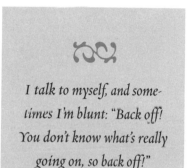

I talk to myself, and sometimes I'm blunt: "Back off! You don't know what's really going on, so back off!"

♥ *Take ten.*

Or twelve or fifteen. Sometimes stress can cause us to explode, and that can be *so* embarrassing! Especially if it happens when others are watching and listening! The old "count to ten" is a great idea, as is a ten-minute break. We've probably all had experiences when we waited (counting or not) and have been so thankful . . . we didn't see the whole picture at first and would have responded inappropriately. I talk to myself, and sometimes I'm blunt: "Back off! You don't know what's really going on, so back off!"

❤ *Laugh!*

Oh, what a difference this can make when you're stressed out! If you tend to take yourself too seriously, recruit help. Call or visit a friend or family member who makes you laugh. And share your funny things with others—it may lift their spirits just when they need it most.

❤ *Participate regularly in activities that are relaxing to you.*

My sister Ann has told me over and over about how wonderful yoga is, so when I saw a little book about yoga a few years ago, I bought it. I can already tell the difference. And one of these days I'm going to read the book! Seriously, find activities in which you can participate regularly such as yoga, tennis, cooking, walking, playing the piano, lying in a hammock, doing crafts, reading . . . something that will help drain the stress away. My niece Wendy suggested that when I'm having trouble relaxing I could try to lie down,

You may want to write down as much as you can about a very stressful event and then shred it. The very act of writing can help to release some of the pain and distress.

get comfortable, and then pretend I'm an ice cube melting! Try that one and see what you think.

♥ *Write things down.*

Keeping a journal can be helpful and healthy. You can record experiences, ideas, and feelings.

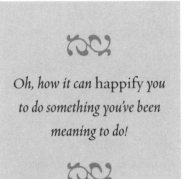

Oh, how it can happify *you to do something you've been meaning to do!*

You may want to write down as much as you can about a very stressful event and then shred it. The very act of writing can help to release some of the pain and distress. Perhaps writing a letter would work better for you, even if you never send it.

♥ *Spend some time with music.*

Have you found some music that unties the knots and calms you down? See if you can have times when "your kind of music" is playing (in your car, home, office, or wherever).

♥ *Do something you've been meaning to do.*

Maybe some of these ideas have come to you as you've been reading this long list. Is there a friend you need to get in touch with? Is there a card you've been meaning to send, a phone call you want to make, a family member you need to forgive? Have you been meaning to tell someone you love them who hasn't heard that from you in far too long? Oh, how it can *happify* you to do something you've been meaning to do!

❤ *Reduce debt.*

Avoid the stress of this philosophy: "All I want is a little more than I'll ever get!" For wonderful ideas and great motivation, read again President Gordon B. Hinckley's talk from the October 1998 priesthood session of general conference (see *Ensign,* November 1998, 51). He shared specific suggestions for getting our financial houses in order.

It's good to dream—but I think it's also important to be optimistically realistic.

❤ *Do some planning.*

Being continually disorganized can cause or add to stress. It's helpful to look ahead, to be prepared as much as possible, to have a plan. Writing it down will help you remember.

❤ *Appreciate more than you expect.*

Have you had times when your expectations have been so high that you were bitterly disappointed when things didn't work out as you had hoped? Oh, it's good to dream—but I think it's also important to be optimistically realistic. (I think the two really *can* become comfortable partners.)

❤ *Work!*

Sometimes when I'm about to perish from stress, I go down in my basement (where there is "matter unorganized") and I get to work— hard, wonderful, physical work—and it *really* can lift my spirits! Other times I'll do different kinds of work—mental, for example. Talk about exhausting! But it relieves stress.

♥ *Know your limits.*

Become more aware of what you can and cannot do. This is so important to your physical and mental and even spiritual well-being. President James E. Faust shared wise counsel in the General Young Women's Meeting in March 1998:

"Women today are encouraged by some to have it all: money, travel, marriage, motherhood, and separate careers in the world. For women, the important ingredients for happiness are to forge an identity, serve the Lord, get an education, develop your talents, serve your family, and if possible to have a family of your own. However, you cannot do all these things well at the same time. . . . You cannot be a 100-percent wife, a 100-percent mother, a 100-percent Church worker, a 100-percent career person,

> There are some things you just can't say no to (even though it would really cut down the stress if you could say no to laundry!), but each of us can probably find some ways to trim our busy schedules.

and a 100-percent public-service person at the same time. How can all of these roles be coordinated? I suggest that you can have it sequentially" (*Ensign,* May 1998, 96).

♥ *Say no to requests you cannot reasonably respond to.*

There are some things you just can't say no to (even though it would really cut down the stress if you could say no to laundry!), but each of us can probably find some ways to trim our busy schedules. Most of us have likely said yes to something we knew we didn't have time for, or sufficient energy or other resources equal to the task.

Would you like a sample of creative excuses to help you say no when you need to? As you read these, imagine someone's response. (I'm serious!) What can they say if you tell them you can't help make 500 costumes for the annual pet parade because you're filing newspaper ads?

Have some fun—add your own ideas to this list of great excuses:

—I'm doing my annual dust ball inventory
—I'm counting and measuring all my gray hairs; this is going to take a while
—I'm training for an acronym marathon, lol
—I'm memorizing all the zip codes west of the Mississippi
—I can't say yes to anything until I lose thirty pounds
—I'm organizing my paper clips
—I'm pasting S&H Green Stamps in my little books; it's something I've been meaning to do for such a long time

—I have to floss my guinea pigs' teeth

—I'm still savoring my jet lag

—The ragweed is too high this time of year

—I have to name my flowers

—I'm thinking about having grandchildren (I'm looking for a book with the title *Grandchildren for Dummies*)

—The man on TV told me to stay tuned

—I'm trying to see how long I can go without saying yes—thanks for helping

—I'm attending the grand opening of my neighbor's garage door

—I'm sculpting a frog out of cottage cheese

Well, I know some of those are quite ridiculous, but you need to try one or two just to get the feel of how effective they can be.

Seriously, now (for the briefest moment), here's one statement I have found to be helpful as I have increasingly had to say "sorry, no" to kind invitations: "I would if I could, but I can't."

And I'm reminded again of the wonderful quote from Anne Morrow Lindbergh shared by Elder Neal A. Maxwell: "My life cannot implement in action the demands of all the people to whom my heart responds" (quoted in *The Smallest Part* [Deseret Book, 1973], 46).

As I'm thinking about this I remember my niece Mary telling me about an experience with her little son Cole. She was having a Relief Society presidency meeting at her home, so she asked Cole to please pick up his toys and help her make things nice for the meeting. His response? "No . . . but that was a good idea."

♥ *Greet the day with a song.*

I learned that principle when I was a bird. "Back in the day," as they say, a lot of us got to be Larks, Bluebirds, and Seagulls in Primary. Fun! I think it was when I was a Lark that I learned to "greet the day with a song." I put the suggestion in here because it reminds me of how important the first few minutes of each day are. Maybe you *do* greet the day with a song, or maybe you do something else to start the day out right. Think of something you can do that will help set the tone for the whole day.

Think of something you can do that will help set the tone for the whole day.

Prayer is critical, isn't it? Maybe you get up early enough to go for a walk or do some scripture reading. Alma encouraged his son Helaman to be thankful each morning with these words: "Counsel with the Lord in all thy doings, and he will direct thee for good; yea, when thou liest down at night lie down unto the Lord, that he may watch over you in your sleep; and when thou risest in the morning let thy heart be full of thanks unto God; and if ye do these things, ye shall be lifted up at the last day" (Alma 37:37). Some have suggested that it helps to write down specific things we're thankful for and then keep the list where we can see it during the day.

💗 *Pray.*

Honest, meaningful communication with Heavenly Father can make all the difference in a moment, an hour, a day, a life.

Regular reading, studying, and pondering can help us make more sense of all that is happening, and can increase our ability to handle our challenges.

💗 *Attend the temple.*

Maybe there is not a temple close enough for you to be there very often, but go as often as you can. It is a place of such peace, guidance, and comfort. Even if you just spend some time near the temple, there can be an increased sense of peace and safety.

♥ *Read the scriptures.*

Have you had the experience of opening the scriptures to "any page" and finding something that lifted your spirits or helped answer a question or dilemma? Regular reading, studying, and pondering can help us make more sense of all that is happening, and can increase our ability to handle our challenges.

♥ *Sing or read the words of the hymns.*

Do you have some favorites? One of mine for when I feel stressed, lonely, or discouraged is hymn number 115, "Come, Ye Disconsolate." I even memorized the words to this and other favorite hymns so they're ready when I need them. And there are other wonderful songs besides just the hymns; I used to sing songs to my dad like "Don't Fence Me In" and "Let the Rest of the World Go By" as he was getting closer to going Home.

Seek a priesthood blessing.

There may be times when you need this additional help and comfort. It is a gift that doesn't have to be saved just for when you think you're going to die in the next half hour. Don't hesitate to ask for a blessing when you need it.

Seek and respond to the Spirit.

The gift of the Holy Ghost is an extraordinary blessing for us in a world that sometimes seems increasingly dark and menacing. Read again the words to hymn number 143, "Let the Holy Spirit Guide," to remember all that the Spirit can and will do.

The gift of the Holy Ghost is an extraordinary blessing for us in a world that sometimes seems increasingly dark and menacing.

❧ *Make needed changes.*

At first for this suggestion I just wrote the word *repent.* But then I wondered if that would include everything that we might think of when we consider making some changes in our lives. Certainly there is sweet peace as we repent. And other changes we make in a positive direction (which is what I hope all of the suggestions here promote) can add new joy, hope, and purpose to our days and experiences. Repentance means turning our hearts and wills to God. It denotes a change of mind, a fresh view about God, about oneself, and about the world. (See LDS edition of the King James Bible, Bible Dictionary, "Repentance," p. 760.) Ponder some changes you can make that will bring this change of mind, this fresh view!

❧ *Cast your burdens on the Lord.*

He is the one who invites us to do this. I love the way it's expressed in hymn number 110: "He shall sustain thee." The Savior taught that He would give His disciples the gift of peace—peace of soul, and peace of heart. "Let not your heart be troubled, neither let it be afraid" (John 14:27).

Elder Neal A. Maxwell taught: "When in situations of stress we wonder if there is any more in us to give, we can be comforted to know that God, who knows our capacity perfectly, placed us here to succeed. No one was foreordained to fail or to be wicked. When we have been weighed and found wanting, let us remember that we were measured before and we were found equal to our tasks; and, therefore, let us continue, but with a more determined discipleship. When we feel overwhelmed, let us recall the assurance that God will not overprogram us; he will not press upon us more than we can bear (D&C 50:40)" ("Meeting the Challenges of Today," *Classic Speeches, vol. 1* [BYU Press, 1978], 165).

Read the Signs

HOW WILL YOU KNOW if you're making progress? There are some signs that we're probably managing stress pretty well. They include:

—We make time for our highest priorities (such as prayer, scriptures, family)

—We have a healthy sense of independence and self-reliance

—We have a good sense of humor, especially the ability to laugh at ourselves

—We're able to both relax and sleep naturally

—We're inclined toward cheerfulness, friend-liness, optimism, and charity

—We have the ability to adapt to changes

There are signs, too, that we're not handling stress very well. These might include:

—Emotional outbursts, including road rage
—A frequent sense of hopelessness and discouragement
—A tendency to pull away from friends and family
—A decreased ability to relax, to laugh, to enjoy life

Look at your life carefully and see if you find that you're experiencing almost constant stress. If so, something is missing, and that something might be the Spirit, the Holy Ghost. I know that you may be one of the many people out there facing life circumstances that are extremely stressful and challenging, and carrying burdens that are SO heavy . . .

And yet the Savior asks us to drop our burdens at His feet.

The irony is, when we don't accept the Savior's loving invitation, what we really may be saying is that He didn't do enough for us. We don't trust that His atonement is enough to cover our problems. Is that really what we think?

In summary, as a long-time observer of and participant in stress (and one with some skill in causing it), I've found a few things that make the biggest difference for me. I am much less likely to feel stressed if I'm doing my best with the basics, such as prayer, scripture

I am much less likely to feel stressed if I'm doing my best with the basics, such as prayer, scripture study, temple attendance, service, and such.

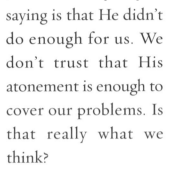

study, temple attendance, service, and such. I've found that when I'm increasingly aware of blessings and am expressing thanks frequently and sincerely, I feel less stress and pressure. It makes a difference for me when I take time to ponder, to meditate. Stress increases if I have an unresolved problem with another person.

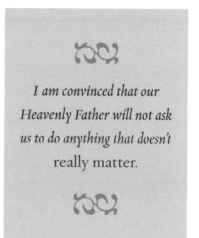

I am convinced that our Heavenly Father will not ask us to do anything that doesn't really matter.

You will find or perhaps already have identified your own ways of dealing with stress. You know the dramatic difference it can make when you're able to deal with the "S" Monsters and other stressors in your life.

I am convinced that our Heavenly Father will not ask us to do anything that doesn't *really matter.* I'm also convinced that our burdens will never be heavier than we can bear if we let our Heavenly Father and the Savior and the Holy Ghost and others help us.

I know that we each have unanswered questions, but I trust that someday our questions will be answered to our complete satisfaction.

So, for a life with much less stress, come unto Christ. Turn to the Savior, *your* Savior. Trust Him. Let Him comfort you, heal you, bring you peace of heart and peace of soul. He *understands* why we get so stressed. He can and will help, not just on some future day, but here and now.

"Wherefore, be of good cheer, and do not fear, for I the Lord am with you, and will stand by you; and ye shall bear record of me, even Jesus Christ, that I am the Son of the living God, that I was, that I am, and that I am to come" (D&C 68:6).

I know He lives. I know He is the living Son of the living God. I know He will come again, and I pray we will be ready to meet Him and to be with Him forever and ever. Our relationship with Him and our Heavenly Father is something no one else can take apart. Walking with Them is the way to keep ourselves together in a pull-apart world.